STRAY DOG EMBASSY

STRAY DOG EMBASSY

NATASHA NUHANOVIC

Mansfield Press

a stuart ross book

Library and Archives Canada Cataloguing in Publication

Nuhanovic, Natasha, 1984-
Stray dog embassy / Natasha Nuhanovic.

Poems.
ISBN 978-1-894469-51-7

I. Title.

PS8627.U43S87 2010 C811'.6 C2010-905913-1

Editor for the Press: Stuart Ross
Design: Denis De Klerck
Typesetting: Stuart Ross
Cover Photo: Luna Simic
Author Photo: Aci Kum

The publication of *Stray Dog Embassy* has been generously supported by the Canada Council for the Arts and the Ontario Arts Council.

ONTARIO ARTS COUNCIL
CONSEIL DES ARTS DE L'ONTARIO

Canada Council for the Arts
Conseil des Arts du Canada

Mansfield Press Inc.
25 Mansfield Avenue, Toronto, Ontario, Canada M6J 2A9
Publisher: Denis De Klerck
www.mansfieldpress.net

Contents

For Snowman

"Once the realization is accepted that even between the closest human beings infinite distances continue, a wonderful living side by side can grow, if they succeed in loving the distance between them which makes it possible for each to see the other whole against the sky."

Rainer Maria Rilke

Rose Deliverer

After I started loving someone, heads of roses
began arriving at my apartment door
instead of the morning paper.

I face my sorrow every time your shoulder
moves away from me when you reach for the lighter.
The butane in my eyes prevents me
from seeing you limping in new shoes
full of brick pieces from your burnt house.

There is no more water.
There are only your slow steps moving
towards the dry kitchen through a smoke-filled city,
an empty canister in your hand.

If I had to learn how to survive without water,
I would rip the heads off roses first
before they die in the smoke,
my shadow told me
through a field of burnt stems,
an empty glass of water in his hand.

There are too many
dried rose heads leaning next to me
but I don't dare touch them with fingers
that smell of gasoline.

Maybe people will open
their morning paper one day and notice
my fingerprints on the last page
that smells of roses, but I don't know.

Revolution in the Hospital

Nothing is wrong with me,
everything is wrong with the others,
in this country of mumbling iron beds
where hospital prisoners trade sheets warm as sunset
for a journey through morphine landscapes.

Every time I have a headache she comes with sedatives—
a new dose of dreaming
as I need it. I am a revolutionary
ready to fight those
who think the history of my illness
is buried in medical texts.

I am still under the sewage oozing from the sleeves of the city
but this is the water I call spring.
My head holds a hidden revolution,
new world rules, where the planet
starts revolving the other way
to remember where I came from.

The sky no longer exists in my pillow.
My morphine dreams no longer exist.
Only my fear of her sneaking through the long corridor
with a silver injection on a silver plate.

The revolution depends on me.
And all I can do now is repeat that
everything is wrong with the others
and nothing is wrong with me.

Stray Dog and Cactus

Nothing remains of my past home
except my bare neck, hairless as a cactus
who chose to belong to no one.
He is the president of my imaginary country,
exiled once he started believing
his skin was never meant to grow needles.

I want to make a nest far from the helmet
of the soldier who died trying to tear down
a fortress of his own medals.
And I limp through the highways inside the asphalt flute
with too many exit holes.

I got hungry on my way to the country
where cacti are shaped like dog smiles
laughing at the map inherited from wolves, my ancestors
who died before showing me the right path.

I finally admitted I would never be a guide dog
leading the blind gardener to the wire fence
where cactus flowers grow,
where the sound of the flute escapes
through more than one hole.

Walking the highway to my new nest on my new paws
and singing old songs about wolves,
I feel the breeze on my collarless neck,
where only one hair remains.
Still I am a cactus
in full bloom.

Family Reunion with God

I met my cousins under my grandfather's grapes
to discuss again the vastness of the cosmos,
the different shapes of God,
while eternity smiled above
our little heads.

All evening we tried to catch up with God.
We didn't see him relaxing on the empty chair
between us, and none of us recognized
his common face.

Then our grandfather became angry.
Our voices were getting too loud for him
to sleep and he sent us all to bed.
He remained, alone. Only God said in a tired voice:
Why the hell does nobody know how to dream!

Climbing Up Stairs

What did I see at the top of the stairs
made from my charred bookshelves?

The ceiling where the chandelier used to be
shines as whole galaxies scream
every time someone flicks a lighter—
an old Ferris wheel bearing broken houses
that are not going anywhere.

I remind myself of one
who never read reports that my house burned down
as I leave my room with nothing
but my broken umbrella. I am
a light bulb with a fractured roof
in the hand I use to ring the bell
on a door that no longer exists.

I have come far, walking
on stairs built on deaths. The rain falls on my head—
a flickering bulb in the library's basement.
Or the start button of the Ferris wheel
filling with water from broken pipes.
But there is nothing to see from the top.
Nothing at all.

If Only a New World

If only we imbeciles had not made barbed wire
out of a child's kite string to separate countries,
if strawberries did not resemble goose bumps
on the cheeks of the guard who couldn't hide his embarrassment,

if the colours on his flag did not dictate
who is guilty and who is a kite,

if even one of us recognized
it is impossible to build a castle
from the ash of a cemetery.

We would not have armies to arrest children
whose marbles would rather become a new planet
than a bullet in the tunnel of history—
just a strawberry stuck in a rifle.

The strawberry might taste like a kite
laughing at the map we drew.
But I am afraid of that.

These Days

The world seems different.

Now I plant tulips in our garden
only to heal your burned lip.

Once you tasted poisoned morning dew.
Once you saw the torn-out flower's stem in my hand.
Once you recognized, in the lines of my palm, my lover's sweat
I did not want to taste.

Sunburnt straw lives in the wedding bed
I turned into a dark, desolate nest.
I have dug up our garden to feed
our seeds to vultures. Even they
would not take anything from my hand.

I am ready to tear out the stars and plant them.
To convince the sun to betray the sky
and glue itself to our dying sunflower that hopes:
Someday I will be different.

And the world would not be so different these days.
And your hand would not bleed when you stroke my soft leg.
And I would no longer sleep beside the homeless.
And I would not hide our wedding ring under my nightgown.
And I would not write you this letter, as you never would.
And pretend not to know why I am different these days.

Different Way

I did not want your winter coat
that still smells like her.

I was afraid I might find in your pocket
chocolate wrappers you used to cover her cold back.

If I could tell you how often I walked
in shoes full of desert sand
over her snow angels diseased by chocolate crumbs
I would not be afraid
to love differently.

If I told you that every time I face your door
I hope it will be locked,

maybe you would not pretend you lost your key
when you spread your arms to make angels in the falling ash.

If I felt your rum breath on my neck
instead of your back kissing my lips,
I would love you in a different way
and let you smell my burned skin
left in your bed to keep your hands away
from the crumpled
chocolate wrappers on your icy floor.

I would love you in that different way
if you recognized my steps
echoing through the hallway.

Shoes full of sand that wake you up, remind you
of the difference
between paper and ash.

Too much smoke is coming from your mouth.
There are so many broken angels in the snow,
you said. Once you love them,
they stay.

I understand why I don't love you in a different way.

My Grandparents' House

for Munevera

The front of my grandparents' house
was destroyed by the grenade that fell
on the house beside theirs.
Exposed brick and a handicapped window ledge
look over their garden where only plastic
flowers remain, keeping shrapnel company in the soil.

But the back is still the same.
Grandmother still looks out her window
hoping for something good to happen.
A freshly painted wall still protects
the hanging mat where I rested as a child
daydreaming about all the different people
I would become.

Lullaby for Dictionary

It is high time I learned the vocabulary of wind, to understand
my fingers coiling into my palm, more like shards
of a vase than a dry flower.
It's about time I learned the secret life of letters in my voice
falling into nobody's dictionary like rain.
All I can do right now is recite my lullaby backwards,
hoping I will remember how to sleep
once I reach the beginning.

Nobody's Anniversary

Can I believe this war has come to an end?
February 29 marks the end of the Sarajevo Siege—
the day doesn't exist this year. Maybe the next.
Am I a coward or an idealist to search
for a formula that will tell me
how to wake up only every four years

on the day when I will not be just
a missing square on the calendar?
But I am what I am—
emptiness in the static on my television,
molecules in my breath that resemble ashes
of eternity. What will I be in my next life?

Once I realize that peace comes slowly
I will no longer remember
endings come even slower.
And the calendar square I wait for
might represent the one life
I will lead differently
from all the others.

Salvia Divinorum

I will never see you again, my overnight happiness
that lasted as long as the Oscar I won,
left by his woman for another man.

If I had your ability to wed tiny water drops
from my Buddha Bar record with a giant waterfall
eating the red carpet I found on the street,
I could be as great as you.

How did you manage to seduce my lips,
ready to kiss three strange men in glowing cloaks?
They pulled me to the floor like Jesus
nailed to the cross. He wanted to call 911,
but forgot where the phone was.

Maybe nothing has remained of the divine insight I gained.
Maybe I am fighting to avoid the place
dull as your burnt remains, which convince me my happiness
is as temporary as a window no one looks out of.

On Forgetting

He killed a doctor
after a doctor killed his mother.
If I knew who I was, I wouldn't ask who all the others are:
killer, doctor, mother,
simple people who inhabit my world with their horror.

Everything is different now, the killer said on the third page,
and the echo of his voice still rocks the fundament of the
park bench
where I used to spend my days.
The doctor was a good man, somebody wrote in the obituary
column.

As she was dying, she thought of her son left at home, the
newspapers said.
The doctor was staring through the window, watching someone
in the park
just watching the day, when something hit him.

If I was more careful, if the mother wasn't dying,
her son wouldn't go to the hospital with flowers
that once used to live in the park.

Now, I sometimes forget
that my favourite bench in the park was once the place
where I measured my happiness.

Night in the Dark Womb

I blow from my lips the smell of my dying country:
I do not want to breathe the smell of sorrow.

Maybe if you hide my earlobe with the same teeth
that pull tight a bandage over the bleeding wrist
of a dying man on the street,
I will forget I have anything to do with the place
I left.

Weave a string of coconuts from a place far away
through the centre of my palms.
Give me the biography nobody wants.
A story about the place I came from,
the stranger,
my stranger.

I want my skirt wrapped around your head,
wounded by the sound of a train rolling over autumn leaves
not ready yet to become part of history.

Am I dreaming I can heal your wound,
perfume your hair growing out of the earth
in the phantom country?

You should have known I lied
when I said I would no longer love you
after you helped me forget my country.

Now my hair is beginning
to smell like a lost scarf hiding in
the hollow shell of a coconut.

A Prisoner's Thoughts

The time is almost here
and I am afraid.

I will forsake my walls of concrete,
my chalk lines counting heavy mornings.
They multiply like pale faces
whose eyes resemble streetlights
blinking at the thought of freedom.

The guard is here
and I am afraid.

He is opening the prison gate.
I no longer feel like going home.
The streetlights are the eyes
of a cat who can no longer see in the dark.
And I am a stranger casting another shadow
on her way to the mysteries outside.

Lonely Milk

I met a talking cow who told me
her mute owner had started
a new diet.

I could tell she was a foreigner and not from the EU
by the bell around her neck—handmade
from dead people's old coats instead of from gold.
She says they are a better compass.

She says she crossed the border illegally
after her current owner bought her
in exchange for his old belt
(he doesn't need it since he gained some weight).

She doesn't speak the same language
as his other cows, who are legal citizens.
Each night she tries to find the border again
before her owner finds her,
night after night,
and yells at her with a milk moustache that smells only of her,
morning after morning.

Bedroom Airplane Crash

My touch has become cold
as the microwave dinner a stewardess forgot to warm up.
My oxygen mask falls from the bedroom ceiling.

I am that stewardess who noticed the sky
is a police station parking lot.
I turned myself in
because of a stranger's hand beside mine.

Before I recognize the date on my plane ticket
mirrors my date of birth,
before I notice I use the same language as the safety brochures:
I might find the life vest
and think about the emergency door.

Instead I will leave on a slow train
and enjoy my time, making a paper airplane
that will fly further than the parachute
made of a pillowcase soaked with
a life I have long outgrown.

Waiting for Sundays

I have eaten all the snow
in the churchyard, sticky as bitter marmalade,
dull as my memory of searching for myself
in places I am trying to forget.

I hid in church benches, a candle holder, an icon frame,
the voice of a choir singer,
to get into that long-dry riverbed and hear pebbles
discuss the spring.
Everybody talked about clouds but nobody mentioned
the old forgotten sky that shakes like a beggar.

It is not my fault the eyes reading the pages
of the Bible remind me of hungry rats
escaped from the cellar.
Nothing remains there except the nightmares of priests
sleeping in their coffins.
They are still searching for that bastard who woke them up
when holy water leaked from their dreams.

I am not the one who was there every Sunday.
Nor the one who will ever know the difference between
water in my memories dripping from an icicle
and water boiling in the baptism bowl.

I am simply an aged man who used to be a boy
looking for Mondays in Sundays
when all the people I knew became footprints
in deep white snow.

Letter Without a Date

You were drinking the loneliness
from the coffee cup that sat on my brown-spattered letter
asking if you are still alive.
I wish you warm coffee, my love.

Did you forget to write the date
on the blank page you send me every month
along with a cheque that makes bank clerks
wonder why the amount is replaced by the words “Still alive”?

The other day the bus driver asked if I will ever pay
my fare on the way back from the cemetery
where I visit grave stones with your name
and I offered him your cheque.
He let me ride because I looked like you.

My apartment seems lonelier every time I get back home.
November wishes me good night,
December wishes me good morning.
The rusty mailbox still bites my hand
every time I reach for emptiness
and find your letter.

No One Recognized Me

I used to love the airport
until I realized planes never take you anywhere.
After so many years I arrived home,
but my own father didn't recognize me
dressed in the feather coat.
No one recognized me.

I still wait at the airport,
watching people push carts stacked
with layers of dead birds.
They smile to the exit the same way
I watch my past.

Still I pretend
to be the same girl with chocolate milk on her lips
who wouldn't go to sleep
before her father read her Peter Pan.

When my father is done reading,
he closes the book and leaves as I disappear
from a world where planes are more
than simply seagulls in a Museum of Natural History.
Maybe my father wishes to see my arms grow feathers after all
or maybe it's just about time
to bury the book in me.

He never came back
and neither did I.

I will never open that book again, but I carry
it with me all the time, afraid that Peter Pan
won't recognize me.
And neither will I recognize him

as I sit stuck in the airport,
watching people
pass me by.

Inside a Crystal Ball

Innocence lies in every end.
Innocence lies in every beginning.
And I am everywhere in between
counting the dots on ladybugs
wondering what they have to do with me.

Ugly Man Dying

He made me think
about that fine line between ugliness and beauty
while he wasted his nights looking for
a cure for a face that passersby fled from.

The surgeon urged him to face the scalpel,
the preacher recommended prayer
and a witch advised him to plant special night seeds
in the ashes of a photograph from his youth.

But even a flower declined to bloom in his presence.
A nobody always gives birth to nothing, he was thinking.
I always worked alone
to avoid hearing other nurses call me
the black nurse who never blooms.
The dry petals in the water tube of his life machine are
growing weaker,
the sound in his throat is worse than a telephone call no
one answers.
Still I pretend not to understand why he feeds his pills
to the dying night flowers beside his bed.

My face is the last face he saw on his way to the place
where I am not yet allowed to go.

After the surgeon left the room smiling,
after the preacher recited a short prayer and ran,
after the witch placed a chunk of soil on his bed,
I watched the flowers suddenly bloom in the vase.

Imagining Paperboys

If only I could believe in the morning horoscope I write
telling me my old life will come back.

People who used to inhabit my days look strangely at
the eyes that turn towards the future
like a deflated ball on its way to the garbage.

I am an astrologist who reads from the wrinkles in my shirt,
but never drowned in a hallucination.
My only goal is to rewrite my own history
with something else as my destiny.

I write my future every time I swallow a grain of detergent
that becomes too heavy, pulling me
into the same ground from which I try to fly away.
Night after night,
morning comes with the paperboy
who walks so gently
I think somebody is knocking on my door.

What Happens to Snowflakes

Our apartment is so small, we cannot pass
each other in the hallway without hugging
in the same way snowflakes kiss
without worrying about their future.

The snowman whose eyes are disappearing in the snow
stares at our window
making sure no one holds the other's hand
too long.

His eyes remind me of the last pyjama button under my neck—
the one you cannot open.

There are too many snowflakes under our tongues,
but just a few hiding from us under our bed.

They resist meeting our hands—
hands capable only of making a snowman—
instead of admiring each snowflake
drifting outside our home.

My Friend Called Time

My mother and my father were worried I was too shy
so they gave me a watch for my birthday.
They said I would do well
to try and get to know Time.

They said to be careful not to define him by the leather strap
that made him look like a cool biker
who could drive me as far as Saturn.

Or by his hands that repeated the same job every day
to pay for the diamonds on his fingernails.

The glass lens was his protection.
He was shy himself and touching the dial
was the only way to hold his hands.

We went everywhere together and became best friends.
When he died I cried for days.
His body remained on my wrist for years.
More days and years passed until I finally recognized
my friend Time in the white stripe
he left on my skin.

Black Cat's Ballad

I am not the one who hides the bullets
in the socks made of thread I stole from hunters.
They use it to prevent escaped tigers
from sleeping in their tents.
I bury the socks in my broken cupboard mirror
and wonder,

Did I pull the trigger?

Did I scare away the tender black cat I was?
Why did I run as soon as my eyes
became bigger than the night that hid the mines?

The dark was once just empty space.
Now it hides the tent rope I stole
to make socks for my wounded paws.
Too ignorant to believe in minefields.
Too afraid to believe in a wound's precision.

No, I used the socks for nothing else,
I pretend as they sway between my teeth,
stuffed with the shards of my broken mirror.

No, I did not pull the trigger.

Empty Wishing Well

Collecting pennies has become
my profession.

I no longer recognize myself in the
gentle steps of a monkey walking out of the dark
confessional booth.
I am afraid he will remember
the donation bin of his church
catching my hand as soon as I learned
how to forget I stole someone else's salvation.

Night has become my companion in crime.
We swim in a wishing well, fishing for pennies.
Sometimes I am still haunted
by their rust biting at my guilty pockets
that try to exchange someone else's desire
for my own.

On my way home,
I gather the savings of a homeless man
right before dawn. His eyes are too sleepy to hide
from the day when he collects bread from pigeons.

I am ready to forsake heaven,
steal from a homeless man,
only to find enough pennies
for a taxi that never stops for me.

But you are too far away.

Where Are You Going?

My breath is a frozen cloud, my eyes a frozen lake.
My voice is a ferry full of ghost passengers going nowhere.
I am the clerk who collects one-way tickets, the captain who drives
from here to there and back to the nameless island.
Every time I tell you no ticket has been sold
you ask what is wrong with the passengers
instead of asking what is wrong with the boat.

I do my best to make wind talkative
in my room of solitude and unasked questions,
on this planet where even ghost stowaways have their own republic.
They celebrate anniversaries with firecrackers that sound like waves.

Sometimes when I see my wound reflected in the lake,
when moonlight grows bigger than my memory of you
and life seems longer than the short memory of my past,
I hear you walk across the frozen lake in my slippers.

You smell of my pyjamas, I smell of foamy shores,
but you were too far to hear me
asking cracks in the ice not to hurt you
on your return.

But the wind always scatters the shadows
of ticketless ghost passengers onto the docks
and everybody wants to go somewhere.
But only one person waits.

Who I Became

When I died I noticed
layers of lives I could have lived better still
resided beneath the fingernails
I'd used to peel away all my mistakes.

Day Before the War

It has become so cold outside that the rain
freezes in the air and turns into prison bars
heavier than those my father carried
at the beginning of the war.

To save the Earth
I burn moments of understanding and moments of horror
at the same time, hoping to create
a staircase to my mother's warm kitchen
instead of the demolished Mostar Bridge.

But the sky runs grey faster
than I can put on shoes I have long outgrown,
and the clouds are soaked with centuries of sorrow
ready to turn the sky into bars—those
that broke my father's back.

Packages for Myself

Packages keep coming back from you,
slowed by the washing-machine gear,
accelerated by your breath, which smells of old oranges.

Your hat, stained with my fingerprints,
floats over the street where I still live.
There the stuck hands of the dead clock,
rather than holding on to the neon wall,
hug my need to write you about it.

I am learning how to be a shadow with sawn lips
whenever my packages to you are returned.
But I would like to forget that the stamps I used
reminded me of orange peels.

Walking Backwards

The loose thread in my shirt
grows inside streets in the burning city.
Its skyscrapers look like tired window washers who never
climbed high enough to clean my fate.

My bones lie scattered between the sound of my hallway
                                                                                                    light switch
and the car brakes I did not push in time.
I bought them from a mechanic trained as a psychic.
He promised if I drove quickly in reverse,
I would beat time and manage to go back.

But the skyscraper I lived in is a place I no longer wish to visit.
My car still stays up at night praying to become a time machine
put together by a monk whose factory
is the imagination of eternity.

The space in between is where I remain
leafing through astral travel booklets intended to comfort me
by saying that everything is as it should be.

Conversations with My Guardian Angel

I am a tiny
ink blot on undeveloped film
failing to capture the moment of happiness
I threw into a garbage basket.

Still, happiness speaks to me
through the voice
of the morning streetcar cleaner,
my guardian angel
who focuses her telescope
trying to find me.

She must wonder why I spend all night
walking through a foggy mirror
worrying when I will learn what I came here for
instead of noticing
I am here only to wonder.

I Am Not

I am not my beliefs.
They are dirt on my windshield from the truck in front of me.
It will fade away with the next rain.

I am not my palm.
That is my map.

I am not my past.
That is my cracked rearview mirror.

Neither am I the sentences I speak.
They are strange hitchhikers I pick up on the way.

I am not my profession.
That is the city I am in right now.

I am the radio that changes stations
when the car drives over a bump,
curious about what I will find somewhere else.

Short Poem About Theft

I am afraid to admit
I am starting to recognize the two of us
from a Bonnie and Clyde hit and run.
Only we are stealing each other's caresses
instead of money, hoping to collect enough
to buy a house with two bedrooms.

Dream Machine on the Highway

I was going the wrong way
after my car spun on the highway.
The sound of the rotating Dream Machine I bought
reminded me of my coughing engine—I still
don't know where to go.

The sound in my head is that of a failed busker
whose music sounds similar
to God's empty plastic bag fluttering in the wind.
He must have come to a closed grocery store
where I never arrived to work one day.

I was too tired from my night job as a prostitute,
wondering why the pole inside the Dream Machine
has become my dancing partner.

The lamp on top of the pole shines like
the headlights of the car ahead of me.
They are my angel's flashlights
reminding me to pick up her laundry
freezing in the draft of my wheel turning
as many times as I change my dreams.

Then I turned and decided where to go.

House of Cards Falling

The bottom row is made of hearts
that resemble my eyelids—shrivelled balloons
trapped in a slot machine. I am one of them,
waiting for a jackpot to release me from myself.

Maybe I could simply leave and witness my house
tumble to the ground—matches or firewood
ready to evaporate. I am one of them,
searching for that buried joker
who will help me to rebuild again.

Walk on the Milky Way

I leave behind me the prints of a camel
attempting to walk on ice—
the echo of a rusty tin box amid a symphony of cellos.

I know nothing about the things I do,
yet it seems
the dirt in my pockets turns into magic stardust

only when I try the impossible.

Then I happily let it seep through my hands,
covering every new place I go
like the worn-out coat I left embracing a chair
in some unfamiliar restaurant.

Stairway to Nowhere

1. I enter.
2. Old messages on the walls.
3. Some happy. More sad.
4. Press the button to my apartment.
5. It doesn't light up, yet it works.
6. On one side a mirror to check how I look.
7. On the other a window to check how the others look.
8. Nobody there for five floors.
9. Someone's grandfather flashes past.
10. He must have not pressed his button on time.
11. Elevator stops after another five floors.
12. A woman with a child enters.
13. The child reads both the sad and the happy messages.
14. He doesn't forget to give me a smile.
15. Elevator stops. They exit.
16. I guess they wanted to go the other way.
17. Long ride up to the 19th floor with nobody there.
18. I exit one floor sooner.
19. This time I have to face only the echo of my own steps
    walking up the stairs.

A Thousand Eyes

The hundred faces I carry with me
are heavy as grey walls,
more silent than peaceful elephants.
If I had a foundation I would rest my head on the earth
but instead I go on counting and know
if I had a trunk I would grab the overripe cherry
on top of the tree just to hold on to something,
even if it was black as my pocket full of strangers.

Just Passing By

The drugs served to me
at an A-List celebrity after-party in Los Angeles
seem so tempting in the shape of a Lotus Flower
explaining to me sacred geometry.

The Lotus Flower resembles my own head
growing in contradictory directions:
Thoughts I let roll past me like credits.
Possibilities I line up before me.

Each one carries a tiny dove in its pocket.
A promise that stopped believing in promises.
Instead it believes in darkness that commits to nothing.

Here only my own shadow made from a rainbow
remains, sacred flower petals decorating its teeth,
reminding me of all the dreams I had
that came to nothing but grey stars in my ashtray.

Working-Class Blues

My voice is a record on the wrong turntable.
Someone else's script lives on my tongue.

I spoke about the number of victims in my city.
And nobody told me why I have age spots
from seeing people die as quickly as my first out-of-body
experience disguised as a dream in God's pyjamas.

In the factory I learned how to deliver a speech about electricity.
I should have spent more time thinking about
why sorrow leaves as slowly as I do.

Then I remembered to connect Canada with Bosnia,
hoping my grandmother's garden sprinkler
would clean the lines on my tongue
that make me speak of the meaningless,
but it was no use.
God is already snoring.

Do Skies Ever Die?

What happened with the sky? The stars are gone
and there is no light to guide me home.

The ash my eyes left was the only ash wishing me goodbye,
as I set sail on a paper boat made of torn-out pages
of my biography I was not yet ready to read.
It will take ages before I realize I am in a box.
I don't ask why.

What happened to me, who increasingly looks like
the traces of my untied shoelaces
in the earth, in the soil
that once used to be the sky?
The only trace was the one left by shooting stars.

Strange Things Happen

In my next life I will live inside a kaleidoscope.

Here streetlights resemble a disco ball and the only car I drive
is a bumper car that never gets lost and never
arrives at the same place.

Bunny ears grow instead of blades of grass—
our planet deciding to change her hairstyle.

Silhouettes of people I knew long ago swim in the sky,
weave strings that look
a little like coming, a little like going.

In this place I understand they are all
just balloons that slipped through the hand
of a little child as soon as something else
became more interesting for a moment.

My Testimony

for my parents

In this mute old war film
with subtitles written by a death-camp guard
I am the voice of peace
once I learn how to speak.

The child's teeth buried in the earth are mine.
They bite the wallpaper of my burning room, scream at my failure
the way the elevator to the top floor howls
like a drowning turtle
struggling to become an alligator.

I left my home too early to understand
my shoelaces might become fancy bows on a politician's neck.
They breathe toothpaste commercials
only to hide the stench of their crowns.
Their hands are the rotting door handles
on my abandoned home.

One war follows another. And I walk mute
along that barbed-wire border.
If I had stayed there
would I find the way to open the old door
with the old key that gasps
on a foreign keychain?
I told my father I embraced my new country
so he'd think I believed his story
where locks look as warm as a turtle's belly.

But this is just the testimony
of someone who does not yet know

if the turtle will grow into
an alligator that will witness
the war that witnesses me.

Acknowledgements

Every person who has shared with me even one moment has fingerprints in this book.

Many of these poems would not have existed without Goran Simic, whose creative viewpoint only made me that much closer to my own and who helped me create a place of understanding, kindness and home. Shaun Kaser is one of the dear friends with whom I shared many beautiful, compassionate and gentle moments. Schien Dong has been a tender support whenever I needed a home between my jumps across lives. Stephen Edwards, Dina Cvjeticanin, Mehreen Rashid, Namam Palander, Nelofar and Zana Talijan have enriched my life with their friendship when I most needed it—from the very beginning of my move to Canada. Special mention to my friends, whom I consider my family, Katja, Hannelore and Gisbert Hofmann. Much appreciation to my family who is still in former Yugoslavia—one of the pieces that seems like a dream I never really recollected properly. I also want to express my deep gratitude to Gary Draper, who saw some of my poems five years ago and was the first to think I had the courage and sensitivity to walk this path. Many thanks to my editor, Stuart Ross, and publisher, Denis De Klerck, for embracing this book with diligence, heart and detail. If I had to acknowledge every dear person that contributed to this book, this section would be longer than my poems.

Last (and first), thanks to my parents, Snezana and Refik Nuhanovic, who were always a loving support and warm place from the beginning and who, every time I left, came with me.

Natasha Nuhanovic was born in 1984 in Zagreb, Croatia. At nine, she moved to Germany, and at fourteen, to Canada. Natasha completed an Honours B.A. in English and German Literature at the University of Waterloo and an M.A. in Comparative Literature at the University of Toronto. Her poems have been published in literary journals in Germany, Bosnia and Canada, and in the chapbook *Painted Photographs* (2005). She has translated poems from and into German, English and Serbo-Croatian. *Stray Dog Embassy* is her first full-length book.

OTHER BOOKS FROM MANSFIELD PRESS

POETRY

Stephen Brockwell & Stuart Ross, eds., *Rogue Stimulus: The Stephen Harper Holiday Anthology for a Prorogued Parliament*
Diana Fitzgerald Bryden, *Learning Russian*
Alice Burdick, *Flutter*
Margaret Christakos, *wipe.under.a.love*
Pino Coluccio, *First Comes Love*
Gary Michael Dault, *The Milk of Birds*
Pier Giorgio Di Cicco, *Early Works*
Christopher Doda, *Aesthetics Lesson*
Rishma Dunlop, *Metropolis*
Jason Heroux, *Emergency Hallelujah*
Jeanette Lynes, *The Aging Cheerleader's Alphabet*
David W. McFadden, *Be Calm, Honey*
Leigh Nash, *Goodbye, Ukulele*
Lillian Necakov, *The Bone Broker*
Peter Norman, *At the Gates of the Theme Park*
Catherine Owen & Joe Rosenblatt, with Karen Moe, *Dog*
Corrado Paina, *Souls in Plain Clothes*
Jim Smith, *Back Off, Assassin! New & Selected Poems*
Robert Earl Stewart, *Something Burned Along the Southern Border*
Priscila Uppal, *Winter Sport: Poems*
Steve Venright, *Floors of Enduring Beauty*
Brian Wickers, *Stations of the Lost*

FICTION

Marianne Apostolides, *The Lucky Child*
Kent Nussey, *A Love Supreme*
Tom Walmsley, *Dog Eat Rat*

NON-FICTION

Pier Giorgio Di Cicco, *Municipal Mind*
Amy Lavender Harris, *Imagining Toronto*